DARLING;

Thank you for the ones who never gave up on me
For my best friend for begging to read every line
For everyone who checked my horrid spelling
And for my girl
For being the reason I finally did this

TABLE OF CONTENTS

As you open these pages
Of my heart soul and life
Reading the words I choked out at 2 am
And the words i wrote when i was on top of the world
Know that
Whether you feel like
You're drowning with anchors
Or flying with balloons
Everything will be okay
This was my hope
Now this is yours

ATYCHIPHOBIA

(N)

Everyone has fears
Fear of heights
Fear of loneliness
Fear of death
fear of life
Fear of love
But the worst fear is simply
The fear of yourself
Fear of imperfection
fear of failure
fear of not being good enough
for yourself

LET IT OUT
DON'T HOLD BACK
YOU ONLY LIVE ONCE, HUN
KISS THAT BOY ALREADY
DO IT, MAKE THAT FIRST MOVE
TELL THAT GIRL WHO TALKED ABOUT YOU BEHIND YOUR
BACK
THAT YOU DON'T LIVE TO PLEASE HER
AND THAT YOU DON'T GIVE A SHIT, WHAT SHE THINKS
SCREAM IT TO THE WORLD
THE WORLD IS YOURS FOR THE TAKING
YOU JUST HAVE TO TAKE THAT FIRST STEP

WE TAKE 12-20 YEARS OF SCHOOL
JUST TO LEARN HOW TO MEMORIZE, TEST, AND FORGET
WHAT EVER HAPPENED TO HAVING AN IMAGINATION?
WHAT EVER HAPPENED TO BEING UNIQUE?
SO MANY YEARS OF "LEARNING"
YET NO ONE EVER DARED TO TEACH US
HOW TO LOVE OURSELVES

SHE GREW UP ONLY HEARING THE WORDS
"THAT IS IMPOSSIBLE"
"YOU'LL FAIL"
"YOU AREN'T GOOD ENOUGH"
SHE GREW UP
TOOK THE "IM" OUT OF IMPOSSIBLE
REPLACED THE FAIL FOR FLY
ERASED THE "N'T" IN AREN'T
AND AGAINST ALL ODDS
SHE PROVED THEM WRONG

SOMETIMES
You are going to make mistakes
Sometimes
You're going to look back and say "what the hell
was wrong with me"
But sometimes
You will look back and say
"I'm the person i am because of that,"
And you'll laugh and shake your head and say
"Who woulda guessed"

I WISH I COULD GO BACK
HOLD THE LITTLE GIRL I USED TO BE
WIPE THE TEARS FROM HER BOILING FACE
TELL HER IT'S GOING TO BE OKAY
TO JUST KEEP HOLDING ON, THAT IT GETS BETTER
BECAUSE WHEN I WAS THAT LITTLE GIRL
THAT WAS ALL I WANTED

WHEN I ACT THE WAY I DO
I DON'T THINK YOU UNDERSTAND WHY
BUT HOW COULD YOU? I DON'T EVEN KNOW MYSELF
WHEN I SAY THE THINGS I SAY
I DON'T THINK YOU UNDERSTAND WHY.
BUT HOW COULD YOU? SOMETIMES I DON'T EVEN
UNDERSTAND MYSELF
SOMEDAYS I DON'T HAVE THE POWER OVER MY HEAD
SOMEDAYS I DON'T HAVE CONTROL OVER MY OWN LEGS
SOMEDAYS
I DON'T KNOW WHO I AM
BUT THOSE SOME DAYS ARE WHEN I NEED YOU MOST

People ALWAYS FEEL THE NEED
TO KEEP EVERYTHING HIDDEN IN THIS WORLD
BECAUSE THEY SIMPLY DON'T WANT TO "BOTHER" OTHERS
OR BECAUSE THEY DON'T SEE IT AS IMPORTANT
BUT WHAT THEY NEED TO HEAR IS THAT
EVERYONE HAS DIFFERENT PAIN TOLERANCES
PHYSICALLY AND MENTALLY
SOME PEOPLE CAN CRY AT THE DROP OF A PEN
SOME STAY SILENT AT FUNERALS
IT'S JUST HOW YOU WERE BUILT
DARLING IT'S PERFECTLY OKAY
TO CRY AT THE DROP OF A PENCIL
IT'S PERFECTLY OKAY TO BE SILENT AT MURDERING NEWS YOU
HAVE THAT RIGHT AS A HUMAN

ISN'T IT FUNNY

HOW THOSE WHO SAY THEY'LL NEVER HURT YOU
END UP HURTING YOU THE MOST
ISN'T IT FUNNY
HOW THOSE WHO SAID THEY'D NEVER LEAVE
TURN THEIR BACKS THE MINUTE THINGS GET HARD
ISN'T IT FUNNY
HOW WE NEVER SEEM TO LEARN
EVEN AFTER BEING HURT MANY TIMES
ISN'T IT FUNNY
HOW WE'D END UP APOLOGIZING
FOR HOW THEY HURT US
YEA FUCKING HILARIOUS

I FLINCH, BUT NOT BECAUSE I'M HURTING OR BECAUSE I WAS HIT GROWING UP, BUT BECAUSE I'M SCARED. BECAUSE I'M SCARED IF YOU GET CLOSE ENOUGH YOU'LL RUN. I'M SCARED IF YOU SEE THE REAL ME YOU WILL TURN AROUND NO MATTER HOW MANY PROMISES YOU'VE MADE TO STAY.

SHE WAS SPECIAL
SHE WALKED THE WORLD WITH HER HEAD HIGH
WITH KNIVES IN HER BACK
POISON IN HER BLOOD
BUT SHE NEVER LET ANYTHING STOP HER
SHE SIMPLY
KEPT
WALKING

16

OH DARLING
YOU ARE A PIECE OF GOLD IN THE WORLD OF STONE

SOMETIMES WORDS CUT ME

LIKE A PIECE OF BROKEN GLASS

THE SCARS STILL LINGER ON THE SURFACE OF MY SKIN

THEY REMIND ME OF WHO I AM AND THE PERSON I HAVE BEEN

SOMEDAYS ARE BETTER

AND OF COURSE SOME DAYS ARE NOT

BUT IT'S GETTING THROUGH THE WORST

REMEMBERING THE BATTLES YOU HAVE FOUGHT

YOU MAY LOSE SOME BATTLES DARLING

ONES YOU'VE FOUGHT HARD BEFORE

BUT KEEP YOUR SWORD READY

CAUSE YOU WILL WIN THE WAR

I WANT TO TELL YOU THAT THEY WON'T LEAVE
I WANT TO TELL YOU THAT THEY WOULD NEVER HURT YOU
BUT DARLING SOME WILL WALK AWAY
SOME WILL STAB YOU IN THE BACK
SOME WILL KICK YOU WHILE YOU'RE DOWN
BUT THE GOOD NEWS IS
SOME WILL STAY
SOME WILL HELP YOU STOP YOUR BLEEDING
SOME WILL HELP YOU GET UP
THEY AREN'T ALL BAD FOR YOU LOVE

YOU JUST HAVE TO PICK YOUR POISON

WHAT YOU NEED TO REMEMBER IS HOW AMAZING YOU
ARE
WHAT YOU NEED TO REMEMBER IS HOW STRONG YOU ARE
WHAT YOU NEED TO REMEMBER IS HOW INTELLIGENT YOU ARE
WHAT YOU NEED TO REMEMBER IS SO MANY PEOPLE LOVE YOU
RIGHT NOW
WHAT YOU NEED TO REMEMBER IS YOU ARE WORTH IT
YOU ARE GOOD ENOUGH
YOU WILL GET THROUGH THIS
YOU NEED TO KNOW THAT
BECAUSE I SURE AS HELL DO

HEY DARING
I LOVE YOU
THAT'S ALL
YOU CAN FLIP THE PAGE NOW

JUST IN CASE YOU NEED IT

I love taking risks
I love doing things that others won't
The high of proving people wrong is something you'll never get
from any drugs
I love saying risky things that make your heart beat out of
your chest
I crave to feel my blood pressure rise after doing something
most would consider crazy
Just love life because you never know when your day is
You could get in a car accident tomorrow
Isn't that crazy to think about
Everything you've ever known could be over
In a second
That's why I love deeply
That's why I act careless
That's why I say I love you
That's why I'm as straightforward as possible
Because you never know
When someone isn't paying attention In the car next to you

YOU'LL BE TOLD THIS ALL YOUR LIFE
EVERYONE IS GOING THROUGH THEIR OWN BATTLES
AND YES THEY ARE
TRUTH IS
WE ALL HAVE A BIT OF HELL IN US
WE EACH HAVE AN OPPORTUNITY TO USE OUR FLAME
TWO WAYS
EITHER IGNITE THE WORLD WITH YOUR LIGHT
OR BURN OTHERS WITH THE HOT BITE

THE FEAR OF IMPERFECTION
THAT RUNS SKIN DEEP WITHIN US
ALWAYS FEELING THE NEED
TO MASK OUR FLAWS
WITH OUR OWN WAYS
BUT DARLING,
THE "FLAWS" YOU SEE IN YOURSELF
THOSE ARE WHAT MAKE YOU
YOU.
AND YOU ARE ONE HELL OF A PIECE OF ART

It's okay to be a mess
It's okay not to know what you're doing with your life
It's okay to have a messy room
It's okay to have a messy head
It's okay to HAVE a messy mess darling

THE MOST BEAUTIFUL THINGS

ARE A MESS

KALON
(N)

I need you to remember something for me, you have only seen yourself 2 ways, in a mirror in and in a photo. Where you are a prop, posing for the reflection. You have never seen yourself when you're laughing so hard you're crying. You have never seen yourself when your eyes are fluttering in your sleep. You have never seen yourself when your eyes light up when doing something you love. You have never seen your natural self. But I have. And I can tell you, you are a masterpiece darling.

I KNOW YOU'RE HURTING
I KNOW YOU FEEL LIKE YOU CAN'T
GO ON
I KNOW YOU FEEL HELPLESS
I KNOW YOU FEEL LIKE GIVING UP
BUT MY GOD
YOU'RE BEAUTIFUL
YOU'RE STRONG
YOU'RE BRILLIANT
DARLING YOU'RE WORTH IT
YOU WILL GET THROUGH THIS HUN
YOU ARE THE EYE OF THE HURRICANE

She was a girl
Who wore her ponytail high
Didn't bother with makeup
And was more than comfortable to go to the
grocery store in sweatpants
She was beautiful simply because she didn't care
Society does not make you beautiful
You make you beautiful

"LISTEN TO ME" SHE SAYS IN A WHISPER WHILE HOLDING HER
BROKEN DAUGHTER IN HER ARMS

"YOU WILL FEEL WORTHLESS SOMETIMES, YOU WILL FEEL LIKE
YOUR BEST WILL NEVER BE ENOUGH, YOU WILL FEEL HOPELESS, A
DISAPPOINTMENT, YOU WILL STOP BELIEVING IN YOURSELF,
YOU WILL WANT TO GIVE UP," SHE TAKES A DEEP BREATH

"BUT DARLING I SEE THAT FIRE IN YOUR EYES THAT BURNS IN
YOUR SOUL. I SEE THAT PASSION YOU WANT TO DRIVE INTO THE
WORLD. I HEAR YOUR WORDS OF KNOWLEDGE AND YOU NEED TO
KNOW YOU ARE STRONG, YOU ARE COURAGEOUS, AND YOU ARE
BRAVE AS HELL. I WILL BELIEVE IN YOU EVERY SINGLE DAY, AND
I WILL TELL YOU IT

UNTIL YOU BELIEVE IT YOURSELF."

YOU CAN'T RELY ON PEOPLE TO MAKE YOU HAPPY

YOU CAN'T RELY ON PEOPLE TO CATCH YOU WHEN YOU FALL

YOU CAN'T RELY ON PEOPLE TO STAY

I GUESS YOU CAN'T REPLY ON PEOPLE

NOT AT ALL

YOU PUSHED PEOPLE AWAY
BUT YOU CAN NEVER ANSWER WHEN THEY ASK YOU WHY
YOU NEVER OPEN UP
BUT CAN NEVER EXPLAIN HOW COME
IT'S JUST HOW YOU WERE RAISED DARLING,
NOTHING TO BE ASHAMED OF

I WISH I COULD EXPLAIN HOW MUCH YOU MEAN TO ME. I WOULD SAY YOU'RE THE REASON THE SUN RISES EVERYDAY BUT THAT ISN'T EVEN CLOSE TO HOW AMAZING YOU ARE. I COULD TELL I LOOK AT YOU LIKE YOU PUT THE STARS IN THE SKY, BUT INSTEAD YOU PUT THE STARS IN MY EYES. I COULD NEVER FORM A SENTENCE USING OUR 26 LETTERS AND COUNTLESS WORDS TO MAKE YOU UNDERSTAND EVEN THE SLIGHTEST HOW MUCH YOU MEAN TO ME.

Somedays
You'll wake up and want to immediately go back
to bed
You'll cover your face with your pillow and
grunt
I want you to do something for yourself
I want you to give yourself a reason to jump out
of bed every day
Give yourself a reason to be excited
Even if it's you promised yourself a donut every
tuesday
You go get your donut darling
You go

I NEVER REALLY UNDERSTOOD
WHY HURRICANES WERE NAMED AFTER PEOPLE
UNTIL YOU WALKED IN
DESTROYING MY LIFE
IN THE MOST BEAUTIFUL WAY
AND NOW I UNDERSTAND
PEOPLE CAN BE JUST AS DESTRUCTION WITH THEIR
WORDS
AS 75 MPH WINDS
BUT THE WORST PART IS
THERE IS NO SHELTER FOR WORDS

YOU ARE A BEAUTIFUL GARDEN
IF ONLY YOU COULD SEE THE VINES GROWING UP YOUR
SPINE
WITH FLOWERS BLOOMING LEFT AND RIGHT
THE WAY YOUR WORDS ROLL OFF YOUR TONGUE
LIKE THE WAVES KISSING THE SHORE
AS SWEET AS FRESHLY PICKED CHERRIES
YOUR EYES AS DEEP AS THE SEA
WITH BEAUTY AND MYSTERY
WITH YOUR HEART BEING THE SUN
THAT MAKES IT ALL HAPPEN

IT'S HELL TO HOLD ON TO SOMETHING POISONOUS
BECAUSE YOU DON'T WANT TO FEEL EMPTY

You hear my story and you think "aww poor you" "I'm so sorry you went through that" but you're only sorry because to you, your life is black and white. Don't be sorry for me for I learned how to love through hurt, to feel through pain, and to see through darkness

SOMETIMES PEOPLE WILL LEAVE YOU AFTER YOU GAVE THEM YOUR EVERYTHING, SOMETIMES PEOPLE WILL BREAK YOUR HEART, SOMETIMES YOUR BEST FRIEND WILL LEAVE YOU AFTER YEARS OF FRIENDSHIP, SOMETIMES PEOPLE WILL STAB YOU IN THE BACK AND ASK WHY YOU'RE BLEEDING, BUT HONEY AT THE END OF THE DAY WHEN YOU'RE CRYING SO HARD YOU CAN'T BREATHE ON YOUR BEDROOM FLOOR AT 2 AM, ALL YOU HAVE IS YOURSELF

AND THAT HAS TO BE ENOUGH. YOU HAVE TO BE ENOUGH.

HER EYES WERE BLUE
RESEMBLING THE OCEAN
LIKE THE ONE SHE DROWNS IN EVERY NIGHT
DEEP AND MYSTERIOUS
DARK AND DANGEROUS

THE WORLD DOES NOT KNOW HOW TO HANDLE
SOMEONE AS AMAZING AS YOU

MY GOD WHAT CAN I DO TO MAKE YOU SEE HOW FUCKING AMAZING YOU ARE. YOU HAVE NOTHING TO LOSE AND EVERYTHING TO GAIN. LOVE, JUST OPEN YOUR EYES AND SEE ALL THAT YOU CAN BE. SMILE, LAUGH, FUCK AROUND WITH YOUR FRIEND JUST DO SOMETHING FOR ME. DO YOUR BEST TO BE HAPPY BECAUSE IF YOU AREN'T THAT WILL BE YOUR BIGGEST REGRET AT THE END OF IT ALL

IF I COULD SHAKE YOU

AND SCREAM

HOW BEAUTIFUL YOU ARE

HOW MUCH THIS WORLD NEEDS YOU

AND JUST STRAIGHT UP HOW BADASS YOU ARE

DON'T THINK FOR A SECOND

I WOULDN'T

THIS IS YOUR LIFE TO LIVE MY DARLING

YOU HAVE ONE SHOT TO LIVE IT

GO OUT

TRAVEL

EAT

DREAM

DO THINGS THAT GIVE YOU A RUSH

DO THE THINGS THAT SCARE THE SHIT OUT OF YOU

DO THE THINGS YOU THOUGHT YOU'D NEVER DO

BECAUSE IF YOU DON'T

IN THE BLINK OF AN EYE YOU'LL HAVE GROWN UP

AND YOU'LL REALIZE

YOU NEVER LIVED

IF YOU HAVEN'T BEEN TOLD YET TODAY

YOU HAVE A BEAUTIFUL SOUL

A BRILLIANT MIND

AND EVERYTHING WILL BE OKAY

Let me tell you a story. Once this little girl who at one time, saw herself as a princess with a crown and all, who began to hear the world's cold words. She did her best to brush them off but eventually she started to listen to them. As she listened her eyes would search the floor as if searching for her younger self, her younger soul. Her crown slipped and broke. She cried and screamed and grew tired. But not the tired sleep and coffee could cure. Oh no. She was tired of the cruel world and thoughts circling her head. She was tired of feelings hopeless, weak, and exhausted. She was tired of being tired. But I can tell you this girl grew not in height but in spirit. When she heard the demons voices she put in headphones and danced and sang. She looked into the mirror she saw the little girl she once was, with her crown and all. She smiled, and put on her crown of her own. She smiled and for the first time in a long time she was proud to be alive. This girl was me. And I am proud of it. I know those days where you feel like giving up, you feel like throwing in the towel, you feel like nothing will never take this pain away. But darling you only see what is right in front of you, you don't see all the amazing things you are going to do. I want you to hold on, look in the mirror, and put that crown on. Because you deserve nothing less.

On those cold nights

When you feel like it's the world against you

Take ten seconds

Breathe in

Breathe out

Get a warm washcloth

Lay it on your forehead

Now do me a favor

Get a piece of paper

And write

And write And write

Because you're writing is the most accurate mirror in the world

beauty isn't skin deep

ANAGAPESIS

(N)

I wanted you

I wanted you so damn bad my bones burned

At the sound of your voice

Your name calmed the white water inside me

But now

My bones are cooled and content

My soul sings a peaceful song with the current

Of my calmed water

The thing about pain is so matter you expect it it still hurts when it hits you. A hurricane is still going to destroy the home no matter how many sandbags you put on your porch

I won't be the first to tell you
That you will fall in love again
I know you think that he is the ONE
And that no one else could possibly fill his shoes
And I know it hurts like nothing else
But darling,
You will meet someone else
It might not be tomorrow or a week from now
He might not have the same brown eyes
But one day you'll see those brown eyes on
someone else
And you'll simply smile

He may have bent you darling,

But he'll never break you

DO YOU NOT KNOW

WHAT "I'LL BE THERE FOR YOU"

FUCKING MEANS?

OH I FORGOT

SILLY ME

YOU'RE ONLY THERE WHEN IT'S CONVENIENT

FOR YOU

The thing about love is it's so common
Yet so rare at the same time
And i really think we could have made it
But our clocks were not aligned

SINCE WHEN DID WE START THROWING AROUND "I LOVE YOU" LIKE
IT WAS HELLO

WHEN DID WE START HAVING SEX WHENEVER IT WAS CONVENIENT

WHEN DID WE START HAVING ANXIETY ATTACKS AND ACT LIKE THEY
WERE NORMAL

WHEN DID SEPARATION BECOME THE GO TO WHEN THINGS GOT
HARD

WHEN DID THE LITTLE THINGS STOP MATTERING

WHEN DID SONGS WITH MEANING BECOME "LAME"

WHEN DID LIFE BECOME JUST FOR BREATHING, NOT LIVING

WHEN DID SOCIAL MEDIA BECOME LATE NIGHT CALLS

WHEN DID RELATIONSHIPS TURN INTO HOOKUPS

WHEN DID FRIENDSHIPS BECOME FRIENDS WITH BENEFITS

WHEN DID THE WORLD CHANGE

AND WHY THE HELL IS IT OKAY

OF COURSE I REMEMBER HIS SMILE
OF COURSE I REMEMBER THE LATE NIGHTS WE WOULD
STAY UP LAUGHING
OF COURSE I REMEMBER HIS LAUGH
OH GOD THAT LAUGH
BUT THE THING IS
THOSE THINGS DON'T STING ME ANYMORE

DON'T YOU DARE COME RUNNING BACK
WHEN I'M FINALLY HAPPY AGAIN
DON'T YOU DARE COME BACK
ACTING LIKE YOU GIVE A SHIT
DON'T YOU DARE FUCKING COME BACK
SAYING YOU MISS ME
BECAUSE WHEN YOU COME RUNNING BACK
I WILL NOT BE THERE

YOU HURT ME
I HOPE YOU HEAR MY NAME
AND IT MAKES YOUR STOMACH CURL
I HOPE YOU SEE MY SMILE
AND YOURS FALLS TO THE FLOOR
YOU HURT ME
THING IS
I'M NOT HURTING ANYMORE
I HOPE LOOK AT ME
INTO MY BRIGHT BLUE EYES
AND I HOPE IT HITS YOU
YOU
FUCKED
UP

BUT MY GOD I WAS WILLING TO FIGHT FOR YOU
I WAS WILLING TO GIVE YOU EVERYTHING I HAD
BUT AT THE END OF THE DAY
THAT JUST WASN'T ENOUGH
I
JUST WASN'T ENOUGH

"IF YOU COULD GO BACK TO THE DAY WE MET, WHAT
WOULD YOU DO?"
SHE SMILES AT HIM
"OH DARLING" SHE WHISPERS AS SHE GRABS HIS SHIRT
"ID TURN AROUND,
AND I WOULD WALK AWAY"

DON'T YOU LOVE IT
WHEN YOU BELIEVE SOMEONE'S DIFFERENT?
WHEN FOR ONCE, YOU WHOLEHEARTEDLY BELIEVE THEY
WON'T LEAVE
WHEN YOU BELIEVE THEY LOVE YOU EVEN WITH ALL YOUR
BAGGAGE
AND RIGHT WHEN YOU BELIEVE THEM
THAT'S THE SECOND THEY CHANGE THEIR MIND.

WHEN HE WALKS AWAY
LET HIM
WHEN HE THREATENS TO LEAVE
LET HIM
JUST PROMISE YOURSELF THIS
WHEN HE FINALLY DOES WALK OUT THAT DOOR
SHUT IT
AND DON'T EVER LOOK BACK

YOU TOLD ME YOU WOULD NEVER LEAVE
YOU TOLD ME YOU'D BE HERE FOR ME TILL THE DAY
AFTER FOREVER
I ASKED IF YOU KNEW WHAT FOREVER MEANT
YOU SAID YES WITH THAT SMILE OF YOURS
6 MONTHS LATER I'M CRYING ON MY BATHROOM FLOOR
I GUESS WE WERE LOOKING AT DIFFERENT
DICTIONARIES

SHE SIGHED
"AND YET I WAS THE ONE WHO TOLD HIM I'D ALWAYS
HERE THERE FOR HIM IF HE NEEDED ME AND HE TOLD ME
HE'S MAKE SURE TO REMEMBER THAT..."
"WHAT HAPPENED AFTER THAT"
"HE LEFT ME ALONE, BROKEN, AND LOST"
HER VOICE WAS BRITTLE
"AND WE HAVEN'T TALKED SINCE"

THIS IS YOUR REMINDER DARLING
YOU ARE LOVED
YOU ARE POWERFUL
AND YOU CAN KICK ASS ON ANY DAY

EVERYONE HANDLES HEARTBREAK DIFFERENTLY
EVERY PERSON'S HEART BREAKS INDIVIDUALLY
SOME HEARTBREAKS WILL LEAVE YOU FEELING
EVERYTHING IS CRASHING DOWN AROUND YOU
SOME WILL MAKE YOU FEEL ABSOLUTELY NOTHING
I DON'T KNOW WHICH ONE IS WORST
DROWNING
OR
DYING OF THIRST

No we may not have ended up together in the end, but you still were a huge part of my life and impact on who I am today. You changed how I saw things. You changed how I saw myself. You made me feel beautiful like no one else. No we may not have ended up together in the end. But it was heaven while it lasted

I GUESS I'M NOT SURPRISED ANYMORE, WHEN PEOPLE
LEAVE THAT IS. ALL THEY EVER DO IS SAY THEY WILL STAY
BUT IT'S ALL TALK NOW A DAYS. "I'LL NEVER HURT YOU"
BULLSHIT AND THE HUNDREDS OF SHATTERED PROMISES
LIE ON THE GROUND IN FRONT OF YOU. I'M NOT
REALLY SURPRISED ANYMORE, WHEN PEOPLE LEAVE I
THINK I'M ACTUALLY MORE SURPRISED WHEN THEY
STAY.

I REMEMBER YOUR DARK EYES LOOKING INTO MINE, BLUE
AND PURE. I REMEMBER HOW YOUR HANDS WOULD GRAZE MY
SKIN AS IF LOOKING FOR SOMETHING. I REMEMBER YOUR
VOICE SOFT AND SWEET TELLING ME WORDS I'D LOVE TO HEAR.
I REMEMBER YOUR LAUGH WHEN WE WERE TALKING AT 2 AM
QUIET SO YOUR PARENTS WOULDN'T HEAR. I REMEMBER
CATCHING YOU STARING AT ME DURING CLASS AND WE'D BOTH
SMIRK AND LOOK AWAY THEN WHEN I ASKED LATER YOU JUST
SMILED AND IGNORED MY QUESTION. NOW I CAN'T LOOK
INTO YOUR EYES BECAUSE THE FIRE THAT BURNS IN MY HEART
WOULD MELT MY BONES NOT THE SAME WAY IT USED TO.
ANYTIME ANOTHER GUY TOUCHES ME I FLINCH REMEMBERING
YOUR TOUCH AND HOW IT ENDED UP BREAKING ME. I NEVER
KNEW YOU COULD MURDER SOMEONE WITHOUT TOUCHING
THEM, UNTIL I SAW YOU STARING AT HER, LIKE YOU USED TO
STARE AT ME

I LIKE BEING COMPLICATED
BEING HARD TO DEAL WITH SOMETIMES
LIKE A PUZZLE
YOU WILL NEVER FIGURE OUT
IT'S HOW I CAN SEE WHO REALLY CARES
IT'S THE ONES TO STICK AROUND
AND TRY TO PUT IT TOGETHER

One of the best feelings in life
Is simply laughing to a point you don't make a
sound
With someone you love and realizing
How lucky you are to have them

SOMETIMES YOU NEED TO FORGIVE THE UNFORGIVABLE
NOT FOR THEM
BUT FOR YOURSELF
FOR YOUR OWN MINDS SAKE
TAKE THE ANCHOR OFF YOUR ANKLE
AS IT FEELS LIKE THE SUN IS PULLING YOU UP TO THE
CLEAR WATER
TAKE THE ANGER OFF YOUR HEART
AND BE ABLE TO KNOW YOUR
PEACE

I WONDER SO MUCH, HOW SOMEONE WHO ONCE CALLED
YOU BEAUTIFUL EVERY MORNING, TOLD YOU THEY
LOVED YOU EVERY NIGHT, AND MADE YOU FEEL SPECIAL,
CAN JUST WALK AWAY. HOW THE HELL CAN SOMEONE
JUST WALK AWAY FROM THAT? KNOWING THEY ARE
LEAVING SOMEONE BROKEN, HURTING, AND FOREVER
QUESTIONING EVERYONE AFTER DOESN'T THAT FUCK
YOU UP A INSIDE A LITTLE?

" WHAT WILL I DO WITHOUT HIM" SHE SOBBED BARELY
BEING ABLE TO SPEAK,

"YOU WILL LIVE MY LOVE, AND YOU WILL LEARN HOW
TO LIVE WITHOUT DEPENDING ON ANYONE BUT
YOURSELF. YOU WILL LEARN TO LOVE YOURSELF, YOUR
BODY, AND YOUR MIND. I NEED YOU TO TAKE THIS
TIME TO LOVE YOU AND ONLY YOU. GRIEVE ALL YOU
WANT TRUST ME THAT'S 100% OKAY, BUT WHEN YOU'VE
LEFT, DON'T TURN BACK"

SOMETIMES PEOPLE WILL LEAVE YOU AFTER YOU GAVE
THEM YOUR EVERYTHING, SOMETIMES PEOPLE WILL
BREAK YOUR HEART, SOMETIMES YOUR BEST FRIEND WILL
LEAVE YOU AFTER YEARS OF FRIENDSHIP, SOMETIMES
PEOPLE WILL STAB YOU IN THE BACK AND ASK WHY
YOU'RE BLEEDING, BUT HONEY AT THE END OF THE DAY
WHEN YOU'RE CRYING SO HARD YOU CAN'T BREATHE ON
YOUR BEDROOM FLOOR AT 2 AM, ALL YOU HAVE IS
YOURSELF
AND THAT HAS TO BE ENOUGH

WHEN SOMEONE OR SOMETHING LEAVES YOU, IT WILL
ALWAYS TAKE A PIECE OF YOU WITH IT. NO MATTER HOW
MANY TIMES YOU TELL YOURSELF IT DIDN'T MATTER,
DARLING IT'S OKAY TO ADMIT IT HURT. ANYTIME YOU
GET ANYTHING REMOVED FROM YOU IT HURTS:
SPLINTERS, BAND AIDS, TEETH, AND OF COURSE A PIECE
OF YOUR HAPPINESS. JUST BECAUSE IT'S NOT A OBJECT
AND YOU CAN'T HOLD IT UP TO OTHERS AND SAY "THIS
IS WHAT IS GONE" DOESN'T NOT MAKE IT ANY LESS
IMPORTANT THAN SOMEONE YOU CAN PUT IN A JAR.
PLEASE DARLING, TAKE YOUR TIME, ICE IT, PUT A
BANDAGE OVER IT TILL IT HEALS. BUT ONCE IT HEALS
YOU GO OUT AND FIND SOMETHING TO PUT IN THAT
EMPTY HOLE, IT MAY NOT FIT PERFECTLY AT FIRST BUT
IT WILL MOLD INTO YOUR BODY.

"DON'T YOU DARE GO TELLING YOUR FRIENDS I WANTED TO
LEAVE YOU, THAT IT WAS MY FIRST CHOICE, THAT I WANTED TO
WALK AWAY" SHE SAYS WITH ANGER IN HER VOICE

"DON'T YOU DARE GO TELLING YOURSELF IT DIDN'T HURT ME
TO WALK AWAY BECAUSE YOU AND I BOTH KNOW IT BROKE ME.
IT TOOK EVERY SINGLE BONE IN MY BODY TO WALK AWAY. IT
WAS THE HARDEST THING I'VE EVER DONE, AND IF YOU
COULDN'T SEE THAT I'M SORRY."

SHE HAS TEARS RUNNING DOWN HER FACE

"BUT THE MORE I STAYED THE LESS I LOVED MYSELF. SO DON'T
YOU EVER SAY I 'WANTED' IT BECAUSE I DIDN'T HAVE A CHOICE,
IT WAS THE ONLY WAY TO SAVE MYSELF."

I will tell you right now,
One of the most painful things you'll ever feel
Is when you realize
Someone who you'd jump in front of a bus for
Wouldn't even press the crosswalk button for
you

YOU, WHOEVER YOU ARE READING THIS. THIS WAS
MEANT FOR YOU. YOU ARE GOING TO GET THROUGH
THIS. REMEMBER WHEN YOU FEEL WEAK YOU ARE
GETTING STRONGER. WHEN YOU FEEL LIKE GIVING UP
REMEMBER EVERYTHING THAT HAS MADE YOU KEEP
GOING. BUT MOST OF ALL REMEMBER YOU ARE
BEAUTIFUL AND YOU ARE LOVED, YOU'RE A BUTTERFLY
DARLING SPREAD YOUR WINGS AND AMAZE THE WORLD.

Sciamachy
(N)

I KNOW YOU'RE TIRED
OF FIGHTING THIS UPHILL BATTLE
I KNOW YOU'RE TIRED
OF FIGHTING THIS ENDLESS WAR
I KNOW YOU'RE TIRED
OF FIGHTING THOSE DARK DEMONS
BUT I NEED YOU TO KEEP FIGHTING
I NEED YOU TO KEEP CLIMBING
MOST OF ALL
I NEED YOU TO KEEP GOING

Hey strong girl
I know you feel like giving up
I know it feels like you have nothing
Left to give
I know it feels like
You'll never be enough
But you don't see what i see
I see the stars in your eyes
I see the ocean in your soul
Mysterious and beautiful
Don't ever change you
Not for anything
Not for anyone

Hey brave boy
I know your battle seems
Unimportant to the world
And to society
I know you feel like
You have to hide your pain
Behind a mask of masculinity
But everyone feels pain
And those who say they don't
Are the ones who feel it the most

"Just tired" she says looking at the floor with
her dull eyes
But look at her
It wasn't a loss of sleep that made her tired
It was a loss of happiness,
A loss of excitement
A loss of hope
And she's waiting for someone to figure that
out

What many don't realize
Is that everyone has their addictions
It might not be alcohol
It might not be drugs
But everyone has an addiction
To numb the pain

HOW I WISH US GIRLS WERE RAISED
TO WATER EACH OTHERS' GARDEN
INSTEAD OF PICKING OUT THE PETALS OF THOSE
AROUND US
WHAT A BEAUTIFUL WORLD WE'D MAKE IF WE STOPPED
COMPETING WITH EACH OTHER

You are you my darling
You embrace those stretch marks
You show off those sassy freckles
You love on your scars
They make you, well, you
And I love you

Don't change for anyone

THERE ARE MANY SAD THINGS IN THE WORLD, TOO MANY TO COUNT. BUT WHAT BREAKS MY HEART THE MOST IS SOMEONE LOOKING INTO THE MIRROR AND NOT LIKING WHAT THEY SEE BACK

"I WISH I COULD CHANGE" SHE SAID AS LOSING HER
VOICE
"BUT SOMETIMES I JUST DON'T FEEL GOOD ENOUGH"

I LOOK INTO THE MIRROR IN SILENCE, BECAUSE THERE'S SO MUCH I WANT TO SAY BUT THERE ARE NO WORDS TO SAY IT. NO WORDS INVENTED TO EXPLAIN THE PAIN OF MY HEART AND THE ACHE OF MY SOUL. SO I SIT IN SILENCE, WITH ONLY MYSELF, AND MY DEMONS

DON'T FORGET
BROKEN GIRLS HAVE SHARP EDGES
THAT TEND TO CUT OTHERS

WHEN PEOPLE ARE HURTING
THEY TEND TO LASH OUT AND HURT OTHERS
NOT BECAUSE THEY WANT TO
BUT WHEN YOU'VE BEEN HURT SO MUCH
YOU TEND NOT TO FEEL ANYTHING
AT ALL

DEPRESSION ISN'T A BEAUTIFUL GIRL SITTING IN FRONT OF
HER MIRROR WITH TEARS RUNNING GRACEFULLY DOWN HER
FACE. IT'S SCREAMING INTO YOUR PILLOW BECAUSE YOU JUST
DON'T KNOW WHAT TO DO ANYMORE, IT'S ANGER
FRUSTRATION IRRITATION AND HATRED FOR YOURSELF AND
THE WORLD, IT'S WANTING TO CRY AT THE DROP OF YOUR
PENCIL. ANXIETY IS NOT A GIRL BITING HER NAILS AND
PLAYING WITH HER HAIR ALL CUTE AT SCHOOL. IT'S SHAKING,
SWEATING AND FEELING LIKE YOU CAN'T BREATHE. ITS
SCREAMING BECAUSE YOU CAN'T FEEL YOUR FINGERS AND YOUR
HEAD HURTS FROM SCREAMING TOO MUCH. MENTAL ILLNESS
SHOULD NEVER BE SEEN AS BEAUTIFUL AND ROMANTIC. ITS
HELL IT'S BREAKING AND HURTING AND IT'S FEELING
HELPLESS. SO WHEN I SAY I HAVE DEPRESSION AND ANXIETY DO
NOT THINK IT'S LIKE THE MOVIES BECAUSE I CAN PROMISE
YOU, IF IT WAS LIKE THE MOVIES EVERYONE WOULD BE
CONSIDERED DEPRESSED

IT'S THE BATTLES SHE FIGHTS AFTER THE SUN GOES
DOWN THAT ARE THE HARDEST
THE ONES OF WHICH SHE FIGHTS TO SAVE HERSELF

"ARE YOU OKAY"

YOUR HEAD ALWAYS BEGIN SPINNING AT THE THOUGHT OF THE
QUESTION. YOUR STOMACH TURNS UPSIDE DOWN AND YOUR
EYES FIND THE FLOOR AS IF SEARCHING FOR THE ANSWER
CARVED INTO THE WOOD. YOU THINK ABOUT HOW YOU SMILE
AT FLOWERS AND POETRY AND YOU LAUGH AT FUNNY JOKES.
HOW YOU STILL MAKE A FOOL OUT OF YOURSELF WHEN NEEDED
AND THAT PART OF YOU IS OKAY. BUT THEN YOU THINK ABOUT
HOW THE STAINS OF YOUR EYELINER WILL FOREVER REMAIN IN
YOUR PILLOW LONG AFTER YOU WASH IT. HOW THE SCREAMS
FROM THE DARKEST HOURS WITH FOREVER ECHO FROM YOUR
WALLS. HOW THE HOLES IN YOUR HEART WILL ALWAYS REMAIN
ABYSSES BECAUSE NOTHING WILL NEVER FILL THEM AND YOU
KNOW THAT. BUT YOU REMEMBER THEY ARE WAITING FOR A
RESPONSE. SO YOU SIMPLY JUST RAISE YOUR HEAD WITH A
SMILE AND SAY

"YEAH WHY WOULDN'T I BE?"

WHEN IN YOUR HEAD YOU'RE SAYING "HOW COULD I BE?"

You think you're slick smiling that bright smile

Laughing your beautiful laugh

But it's in your eyes
I see your storm
Your bloody battles You fight within yourself
I see those moments
When your face drops
Because you think no one is looking
I see those daring eyes
Of yours
But I don't see the fire Like you used to have
But darling
I see your beauty Your grace
And your strength
I see that fight
That passion to win
I know you think the battle is killing you
But as I see it It's making you stronger
I will be be there
Through the whole war

I won't be the first to tell you
That you will fall in love again
I know you think that he is the ONE
And that no one else could possibly fill his shoes
And I know it hurts like nothing else
But darling,
You will meet someone else
It might not be tomorrow or a week from now
He might not have the same brown eyes
But one day you'll see those brown eyes on
someone else
And you'll simply smile
And walk away

WAKE UP EVERY MORNING AND TELL YOURSELF "I WILL GET THROUGH TODAY LIKE I GOT THROUGH YESTERDAY AND LIKE I WILL GET THROUGH TOMORROW"

"HOW WAS YOUR DAY DARLING"

"IT WAS OKAY, HOW WAS YOURS?"

"WHY ONLY OKAY" HE ASKS "YOU HUNG OUT WITH
FRIENDS... YOU SEEMED PRETTY TO HAPPY TO ME."

SHE LOOKS AT HIM WITH A SMILE ON HER FACE BUT
BROKENNESS IN HER EYES, "YOU SEE I COULD TRY TO
EXPLAIN IT, AND YOU COULD TRY TO UNDERSTAND" SHE
TOOK A BREATH

"BUT LOVE, YOU WILL NEVER UNDERSTAND, UNTIL YOU
ARE STANDING IN A ROOM FULL OF PEOPLE, AND YOU
FEEL ALONE"

THERE WILL BE A DAY WHEN YOU FIND SOMEONE, THEY DON'T HAVE TO BE A BOYFRIEND OR A GIRLFRIEND, THEY ARE JUST THE ONE PERSON WHO CAN MAKE YOU LAUGH WHEN YOU WANT TO CRY, THEY CAN CHANGE YOUR VIEW ON THE WORLD, THEY MAKE YOU LOVED WHEN YOU'RE AT YOUR LOWEST. THEY WILL BE YOUR SHOULDER WHEN TEARS ARE FALLING DOWN YOUR FACE, THEY WILL BE YOUR CRUTCH WHEN YOU ARE BROKEN, THEY NEVER LET YOU GO A DAY THINKING YOU'RE UNWANTED. THE ONE WHO MAKES YOU THE BEST YOU CAN BE. THIS PERSON IS YOUR SOULMATE DARLING, DON'T EVER LET THEM GO

SHE LAUGHS SO LOUD, THEY HAVE TO TELL HER TO BE QUIET.

SHE SMILES SO HARD, THEY ASK HER IF HER MOUTH HURTS.

SHE MAKES EVERYONE LAUGH TILL THEY CRY, THEY WONDER HOW SHE DOES IT.

SHE'S SO HAPPY, THEY TELL HER TO CALM DOWN.

BUT WHAT THEY DON'T KNOW IS SHE IS JUST TRYING TO BE LOUDER THAN THE VOICES IN HER HEAD. SHE'S JUST TRYING TO NOT FEEL UPSET FOR JUST A LITTLE BIT, SHE IS TRYING TO FEEL SOMETHING ELSE BESIDES NUMB

HOW DO YOU EXPECT ME TO EXPLAIN WHAT IS
HAPPENING IN MY HEAD WHEN I DON'T EVEN KNOW

THE ANSWER MYSELF

THE THING ABOUT MENTAL ILLNESS IS IT'S SO HARD FOR
PEOPLE TO UNDERSTAND WHAT IT IS BECAUSE THEY CAN'T SEE
IT. THEY CAN'T SEE THE BROKENNESS OF THE SOUL THAT SHREDS
EVERY NIGHT AT THE SOUND OF PARENTS FIGHTING. THEY
CAN'T SEE THE LACK OF COLOR IN YOUR EYE AFTER A LONG
NIGHT OF CRYING YOURSELF TO SLEEP WISHING YOU WOULDN'T
WAKE UP. SO WE GO AROUND LIKE WE ARE NORMAL AND WE
FEEL INSANE FOR HOW WE FEEL BECAUSE NO ONE GETS IT. NO
ONE BOTHERS TO READ BETWEEN THE LINES. IF THEY CAN'T SEE
A CAST OR A TUMOR OR A X RAY IT ISN'T REAL TO THEM
BECAUSE IT DOESN'T HAVE TO BE. BUT MY GOD IT'S SO REAL TO
US. SO FUCKING REAL

YOUR BODY LOVES YOU

ALWAYS REMEMBER THAT BEFORE HURTING IT

YOU WAKE UP EVERYDAY ALIVE EVEN ON THE DAYS YOU DON'T
WANT TO

BECAUSE WHILE YOU WERE SLEEPING

YOUR BODY STAYED AWAKE TO KEEP YOU BREATHING

ALL THOSE CUTS AND SCABS

YOUR BODY WORKED EXTRA TO HEAL YOU

YOU'RE YOUR OWN BIGGEST FAN

BE NICE TO YOURSELF

PLEASE

DO YOU EVER FEEL CRAZY

FOR FEARING WHAT YOU CAN'T SEE

FOR FEARING THE PAST PRESENT AND FUTURE AT THE SAME
TIME

OR THE MONSTER UNDER YOUR BED

DO YOU EVER FEEL CRAZY

FOR FEARING WHAT'S IN YOUR HEAD

One of the most important things you can learn
in life
Is how to love others
When you're feeling the most broken
Giving even the little part to another broken
soul
Can be one of the most filling feelings

THIS WORLD HAS BECOME HOME OF THE BROKEN

THE VOICE OF THOSE WHO WEIGH YOU DOWN WITH
ANCHORS FOR THEIR OWN

THE WORDS OF THOSE PEOPLE WHO LEAVE YOU FEELING
WORTHLESS

AND WORST OF ALL

THE ONE IN YOUR HEAD

YOU KNOW WHICH ONE I'M TALKING ABOUT

SOME DAYS

YOU'LL WANT TO SCREAM AND RIP YOURSELF TO PIECES

SOME DAYS

YOU'LL SPEND HOURS TRYING TO STITCH YOURSELF BACK
TOGETHER

SOME DAYS

YOU WON'T HAVE THE ENERGY TO DO ANYTHING BUT SIMPLY
EXIST

I WANT TO REMIND YOU THAT YOU CAN FUCKING DO
THIS
I DON'T CARE WHAT THOSE DEMONS IN YOUR HEAD SAY
I DON'T CARE WHAT THE DOCTORS TELL YOU
I DON'T CARE WHAT YOUR FRIENDS SAY
YOU ARE GOING TO GET THROUGH THIS
YOU JUST NEED TO KNOW YOU CAN
BECAUSE I KNOW YOU CAN

LATIBULE
(N)

Here is your reminder it's okay,
It's okay if you failed that test you studied hours for, a
test doesn't define your intelligence
It's okay if you're curled up on the floor with tears
streaming down your face because you feel nothing
and everything at the same time, everyone feels things
differently
It's okay if you are screaming into your pillow,
sometimes you just have to let it out
It's okay if you stay in bed for 43 hours straight to
avoid the world, everyone deserves those quiet hours
It's okay if you say you're fine when you're really
breaking inside, you just want to appear strong
And that is okay, it is all okay , it will be okay
You will be okay

You held me, and to you it was just a hug, but to me it was my world. What you didn't know was you were holding a broken girl, what you didn't know is you were holding someone who wanted to give up. What you didn't know is you were holding someone who wanted to end it all. What you didn't know is you saved that girl's life. And while you will never think of that hug again, it's the reason that girl started to believe again.

~THANK YOU MY GIRL

EVERYONE NEEDS THEIR "PERSON"
THE FIRST PERSON YOU GO TO
WHEN ANYTHING BIG HAPPENS
OR ANYTHING HAPPENS AT ALL
THE PERSON YOU THINK OF FIRST
WHEN SOMETHING AMAZING HAPPENS
THE PERSON'S ARMS YOU STUMBLE INTO
WHEN HEART BROKEN
THIS WORLD IS COLD
EVERYONE NEEDS ARMS TO STUMBLE INTO ON COLD NIGHTS

~EVEN THE STRONGEST ONES
-TO YOU BUG

You'll never understand
How much You Mean to me
You will never understand
Without you I wouldn't be here
You'll never understand
You make the war in My head
Calm down for awhile
You will never understand
Your touch calms
the fire in my soul
You will never understand
You make life worth The fight
You will never understand
How much
You mean to me
You don't have to be blood
To be family

Sometimes the world will throw punches at you
And you'll want to throw punches back
But remember
The punches wouldn't be thrown
If you weren't strong enough to take the hit

I think one of the most amazing thing is when
someone has walked through hell with a smile on their
face
I think one of the most amazing things is a person
who has so much pain
Yet all they do is spread love
I think one of the most amazing things is someone
who wears their hearts on their sleeve
After being broken too many times to count
I think of of the most amazing things is you
Please don't change for anything
Or anyone
Be brave love
Be brave

You will meet someone one day,
Who will scare the living hell out of you
They will challenge you
They will love you
They will figure out your little pieces of your puzzle
that you didn't even know existed
And when you get the feeling you want to leave
Don't
You will regret missing out on a lifetime of
adventure
You will regret missing out on finding yourself

Look outside your window
Into the world
Look at the most beautiful things
Whether it's the city skyline
Or the tall pine trees swaying in the wind
They are all so different
Yet they are all beautiful
They are all perfect in their own ways
They don't have anything in common
Yet they are all perfectly imperfect
Like you
You are perfectly imperfect

EVERYONE NEEDS A SAFE PLACE
EVERYONE NEEDS SOMEWHERE
WHERE THEY CAN HIDE FROM THE WORLD
EVERYONE NEEDS A HIDEAWAY

SOME PEOPLE ARE SUPPOSED TO COME AND GO
WITH FEW WORDS SAID
SOME PEOPLE ARE SUPPOSED TO WRITE CHARACTERS
IN YOUR LIFE
BUT YOU NEED TO REMEMBER WHO'S HOLDING THE PEN
WHEN WRITING THE STORY OF YOUR LIFE

SOMETIMES
YOU NEED TO GO FAR AWAY
YOU NEED TO GO RUN AND RUN AND RUN
UNTIL YOUR LEGS GIVE OUT
YOU NEED TO SCREAM SO LOUD YOU CAN'T HEAR YOUR OWN
HEARTBEAT
SOMETIMES YOU JUST NEED TO FEEL
ANYTHING BESIDES NOTHING

No matter how hard you try
You simply cannot save a broken soul
But what you can do
Is love the hell out of them

DO YOU EVER WONDER WHO YOU WOULD BE IF THINGS WERE DIFFERENT? IF THAT BOY HAD LOVED YOU BACK? OR IF YOUR PARENTS WERE HAPPILY MARRIED INSTEAD OF TWO STRANGERS WITH MEMORIES? OR IF YOUR BEST FRIEND DIDN'T STAB YOU IN THE BACK..? WHO WOULD BE WALKING AROUND IN YOUR BODY?

No matter what is happening in your life darling
Promise yourself
That you will never ever
Apologize for doing what was best for you

Now that you have seen every part of me
You have ran your fingers through my deepest secrets
You can read the lines of my darkest corners
I hope this helps you fight your battles
Cause darling
You
Are
Worth it

Made in the USA
Columbia, SC
31 March 2018